GREEK ISLAND MYTHS

KOS
HIPPOCRATES AND ASCLEPIUS

JILL DUDLEY

PUT IT IN YOUR POCKET SERIES
ORPINGTON PUBLISHERS

Published by
Orpington Publishers

Cover design and origination by
Creeds, Bridport, Dorset
01308 423411

Printed and bound in the UK by
Creeds

© Jill Dudley 2016

ISBN: 978-0-9934890-7-5

KOS

HIPPOCRATES AND ASCLEPIUS

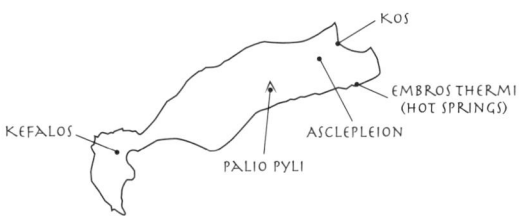

Kos is one of the Dodecanese islands in the south of the Aegean. Its eastern end is mountainous and tree-covered. The port of Kos is alive with activity, its quayside lined with fishing boats, yachts and schooners, with palm trees gracing the roadside. Numerous cyclists take to the cycle paths, and there is a feeling of well-being, good health and energy, which is as it should be on this unique island of Hippocrates, the father of medicine, who lived c.460 B.C.

Kos first became famous as a centre of healing due to its Asclepeion, a three-terraced temenos (sacred enclosure) dedicated to Asclepius, god of healing. He was the son of Apollo. In fact, it had been Apollo who had first been worshipped there. His sanctuary was surrounded by a Holy Grove of cypresses which were considered sacred to him.

He was known on Kos as Apollo Kyparissios (an epithet denoting 'cypress tree'), and it was forbidden to cut down any of the trees within his sacred precinct.

The worship of Apollo then shifted to Asclepius, his son by a mortal woman Coronis. She gave birth to him at Epidaurus* in the Peloponnese, which soon became a renowned centre of healing. There she exposed the baby on a mountainside where he was found by a shepherd who, recognizing the child's divinity from a light that shone about him, took him home where he was protected by his dog and suckled by his goat.

In another story Coronis was unfaithful to him while still pregnant with Asclepius. Apollo was informed of her infidelity by a white crow (at the time all crows were white), and he was so outraged that he killed Coronis (some say Artemis his sister killed her). Apollo rescued his child and entrusted him to Chiron, a centaur (half-man, half-horse) who was renowned throughout the ancient world for his medical knowledge, his music and his justice. Afterwards, Apollo was so filled with remorse at having killed his beloved Coronis, and so furious with the crow for informing against her, that he turned all crows black.

It was thought by many that the worship of Asclepius, this god of healing, had been brought to Kos by the Dorians who had come to the island from Epidaurus. It was, perhaps, the myth of the birth of Asclepius and the death of his mother, that led to the rule of barring anyone from an Asclepeion who was on the point of death or about to give birth.

Before entering the temple at the great Asclepeion on Kos, an invalid had first to go through certain strict procedures. First, he had to fast, then undergo purification, and offer up a sacrifice to the god. Those who could afford nothing greater would bring a cock, others a sheep or a goat. Having done these preliminaries, the patient was expected to take part in a 'temple sleep'. This took place in a long portico where invalids lay side by side. During the night it was hoped that a miraculous cure would take place, or that a dream would be sent by the god informing the patient of the remedy needed to help his recovery. Temple snakes, sacred to Asclepius, were also used; they would slither up and lick a festering wound or skin complaint and so effect a cure. If there was no recovery, then it was from lack of some essential detail to appease the gods.

There must have been countless miraculous recoveries, otherwise patients would never have bothered with all the hassle involved.

Hippocrates was descended from a long line of priest-physicians who served at the Asclepeion, and were known as Asclepiads. His father had been one, and Hippocrates had learned the art of medicine from him. What distinguished Hippocrates, however, was his focus on medicine as a science in itself, and not in any way connected to the displeasure of a god. He believed there was a natural cause to all disease, and he opposed the Asclepiad priest-physicians who held on to the traditional idea that it was the gods who inflicted accidents or diseases on people. 'It is not the god who is to blame' was something Hippocrates insisted repeatedly. What was required, he said, was proper diagnosis, painstaking research into curative medicine, and treatment appropriately given in each individual case.

Where the priest-physicians might have made an incision to let out what they regarded as an evil demon that had gained access to a patient showing mental stress and instability, Hippocrates looked for the causes to mood swings or depression. He could be said to be the first ever psychologist.

His essay, *On Airs, Waters, Places,* was full of fatherly advice and concern, describing how climate and the changing seasons, environment, and diet, all played a part in the good or bad health and well-being of an individual. 'Excess of any kind is an enemy of nature' was one of his maxims.

Hippocrates was a great believer in nature. Nature was untaught and unfailing in itself. 'Nothing arises without its natural cause', was another maxim. He recognized that in every human being there was a vital force and energy at work which kept that person healthy.

Hippocrates' fame spread, and he was in demand throughout the known world. Pericles, the great Athenian statesman of the fifth century B.C., sought his help when Athens* was suffering from the plague. Afterwards Pericles rewarded him at the great Athenian Panathenaea festival by crowning him with a golden wreath, as well as giving him Athenian citizenship which meant free meals for life. Soon after that, an Asclepeion sanctuary was founded in Athens on the south side of the Acropolis.

The Persian king, Artaxerxes, also appealed to Hippocrates because of plague infesting his army. He promised him untold wealth and luxury if he came. Considering the long term enmity between Persia and Greece, it showed a nerve. But Hippocrates was not one to be tempted by riches or comfort, and refused.

It was the Hippocratic Oath which made Hippocrates world famous, and which is still observed by the medical profession today. Its words were: *I swear by Apollo, the Physician, by Asclepius, by Hygiea and Panacea and by all the gods and goddesses, making them my witnesses, that I will carry out, according to my ability and judgement, this oath and this covenant...*

With regard to healing the sick, I will devise and order for them the best diet, according to my judgement and means; and I will take care that they suffer no hurt or damage.

Nor shall any man's entreaty prevail upon me to administer poison to anyone; neither will I counsel any man to do so. Moreover, I will give no sort of medicine to any pregnant woman, with a view to destroy the child...

Whatsoever house I may enter, my visit shall be for the convenience and advantage of the patient; and I will willingly refrain from doing any injury or wrong from falsehood, and (in an especial manner) from acts of an amorous nature, whatever may be the rank of those who it may be my duty to cure, whether mistress or servant, bond or free.

Whatever, in the course of my practice, I may see or hear (even when not invited), whatever I may happen to obtain knowledge of, if it be not proper to repeat it, I will keep sacred and secret within my own breast.

If I faithfully observe this oath, may I thrive and prosper in my fortune and profession, and live in the estimation of posterity; or on breach thereof, may the reverse be my fate.

In the fifth century A.D., the emperor Theodosius II decreed the closure of all pagan sanctuaries, and a Christian church was built on the site of the old Kos Asclepeion. A massive earthquake in 554 A.D. destroyed the site, and for centuries the whole area lay forgotten under layers of alluvium. In the first years of the fourteenth century the Knights of St. John arrived on Kos and again the historic pagan site was Christianized with a church which was dedicated to Our Lady of the Grove. It was not until the early twentieth century that excavations began, and the lost buildings of the ancient Asclepeion were again revealed.

Today on Kos there is an ancient plane tree claimed to be (somewhat dubiously) the very one under which Hippocrates had taught and expounded words of medical wisdom to his devoted followers. It has a massive girth with a wide hollow gash in its trunk as though blasted by lightning. Metal poles support the weight of its branches, and it is surrounded by a protective railing. It grows at the heart of Kos port where many reminders of the island's historic past are to be seen: a Corinthian capital from Roman times; the fourteenth century castle of the Knights of St. John built when the Crusaders had been on the island; an old mosque from the Ottoman era. The street is lined with attractive tall houses with arched windows and arcades from the Italian occupation in the early twentieth century.

One of Hippocrates' famous aphorisms on medicine was: 'Life is short, but the art is long, the opportunity fleeting, the experiment perilous, the judgement difficult.' The great physician died in extreme old age at the end of the fourth century B.C. He was then living in the town of Larissa in northern Greece.

Today on Kos there is an International Hippocratic

Foundation Centre, founded in 1960. It has a medical library, and a museum on the history of medicine.

Medical conferences are held there regularly. It is a fitting tribute to Hippocrates, the father of medicine, and son of a priest-physician who had served Asclepius, the ancient god of healing.

Denotes a separate booklet on the subject.

THE IMMORTAL GODS BORN OF ZEUS BY MORTAL WOMEN

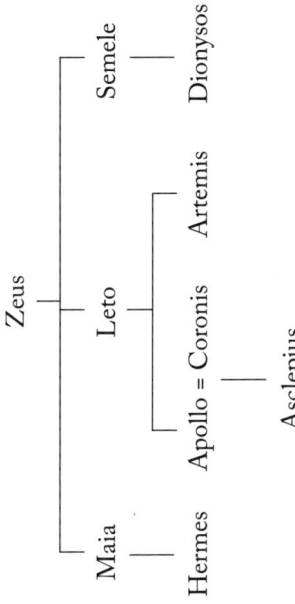

GLOSSARY OF GODS AND GODDESSES

APOLLO – Son of the supreme god Zeus and the mortal woman Leto. He was god of medicine, music, archery and prophecy. He was also god of light, hence his epithet Phoebus meaning 'bright'.

ASCLEPIUS – Son of Apollo by the mortal woman Coronis. He was a god of healing, and the priest-physicians serving him in his temple at Kos were called Asclepiads.

CENTAURS – A race of creatures with the body and legs of a horse, and head and arms of a man. They lived on Mount Pelion in Thessaly.

CHIRON – A Centaur, but a wise and kindly one. He was learned in medicine and the arts, especially music. He became tutor to many famous heroes such as Jason, Achilles and Apollo's son Asclepius.

HYGIEA – Goddess of health, and daughter of Asclepius.

PANACEA – Daughter of Asclepius, from which our word 'panacea', meaning universal remedy, comes.

MORE FROM THE
PUT IT IN YOUR POCKET SERIES
GREEK MYTHS

TROJAN WAR
THE JUDGEMENT OF PARIS
HELEN
KING AGAMEMNON
ACHILLES
THE WOODEN HORSE
ODYSSEUS

SACRED SITES
ATHENS – THE ACROPOLIS
CORINTH – ST. PAUL AND THE GODDESS OF LOVE
DELPHI – THE ORACLE OF APOLLO
ELEUSIS – DEMETER AND KORE
EPIDAURUS – CENTRE OF HEALING
OLYMPIA – THE OLYMPIC GAMES

ALSO BY JILL DUDLEY

YE GODS! (TRAVELS IN GREECE)

YE GODS! II (MORE TRAVELS IN GREECE)

LAP OF THE GODS (TRAVELS IN CRETE
AND THE AEGEAN ISLANDS)